AF264933

LIFE'S REEL

G. Allen

ALSO BY THE AUTHOR

Peeling, Dealing, and Healing

LIFE'S REEL

G. Allen

ISBN: 099839453X
ISBN-13: 978-0998394534

DEDICATION

To the shining stars in my universe

ACKNOWLEDGEMENT

Cover art courtesy of Courtney Leal @hazelmdesigns

CONTENTS

INNER CIRCLE

A Good Book

Let me escape into your pages,

Into that fluid world

Where reality mixes with illusion.

You are the rock I rest upon;

You are the calm in my chaos;

You are my oasis in a scattered world.

A Peaceful Retreat

Morning coffee on my back deck

Nature doing a sound check

I ground myself before the day's trek.

The breeze stirs the moist morning air

Light dances with the trees, laissez faire

I melt into the wrought iron chair.

Wooden boards under my feet

Muffled sounds from the street

I experience a peaceful retreat.

Cotton Top

Baby of the family called Cotton Top

Southern girl

New Orleans born and raised

Full of spirit and charm

An independent '50s woman, smart and sharply dressed

You carry yourself with grace and style

Setting a blueprint for motherhood

Your words of wisdom linger in my ear

Father's Day

Stable and loving, trustworthy and fair,

I try to be like you.

Stubborn, entrenched, sometimes loud and passionate,

Guess I am a lot like you.

I would like to send you a card,

But how would I get it to where you are?

Mail to Heaven is a bit too far.

Four-O'Clocks

I planted four-o'clocks in my garden in memory of my grandmother.

When I was little, she would take me, hand-in-hand, for an evening stroll.

We would stop and pick four-o'clock flowers, threading them on a stalk.

I'd wave my colorful wand as we greeted her stoop-sitting neighbors.

I thought myself a flower princess.

When we returned to her house, she'd store them in the icebox, so they'd last longer.

They never did. By morning, the flowers were closed, wilted, and sad.

Nothing lasts forever.

As I grew, she'd invite me to go with her for an evening stroll and pick four-o'clocks.

I no longer believed in flower princesses, so I declined.

Nothing lasts forever.

I wish she were still here to pick four-o'clocks with me.

Nothing last forever.

The Gilding

Particles of multicolored energy gather close,

The essence of things to come.

Shadows of doubt, now removed, allow them to penetrate the flesh,

Absorbed by the body, molded by the soul.

The alchemy continues, each layer builds upon itself.

Its beauty is transfixing; I'm unable to look away.

Gold, in its purist form, is now your protection.

My Hope for You

Take advantage of every opportunity to become more of the best parts of yourself.

Shine as a guiding star to someone.

Find happiness in the little things and gratitude in the big things.

Be an example of how we should all treat each other.

Find your place in the Universe.

Ode to the Old Farm Woman

Hair in bun and clothes homespun

Length of dress shows time regress

On open stairs, sometimes there

Shards of light can make you bright

Lights are flashing, chairs dashing

Children laughing, ice smashing

Shake the man to farm the land

Make kid cry and fan will fly

She did show so he will know

Kids are gone, and you've moved on

Were you mine or of your time?

Now you're free to stay or flee.

Precious Pearl

When my dad shucked oysters for Thanksgiving
dressing, I would stand close to him,

Hoping to find a pearl in the just-opened bivalves.

I never did find one in those discarded shells.

The one I carry is in my heart,

Formed by a precious memory.

Rainbow Girl

Pronking up the waterfall path,

Through the quilted trees,

Trying to catch the Rainbow Girl,

Hiding in the voile of mist.

She piques my senses,

For she is more attuned than I.

Her evocative nature is unsettlingly,

Reminiscent of someone I once was.

Maybe if I catch her,

She will share her secrets with me.

Remembering Spider Hall Farm

I remember ...

Hearing eggs frying just after dawn.

Learning the names of birds dotting the lawn.

Seeing thunder ignite the sky.

Picking fresh berries for blackberry pie.

Sliding in socks on the polished floor.

Turning the brass handle on the attic door.

Tasting a batch of Jean's strawberry jam.

Drooling over the smell of baked ham.

Looking at the world through bubbled glass.

Spying the geese descend to the grass.

Opening the windows to feel a gust.

Trying to make a perfect pie crust.

Watching the children race down the hill.

Shooting tin cans for a thrill.

Going to the garden to cut fresh greens.

Smelling the rain hitting the screens.

Making a wreath from gathered boxwood.

Crossing the field to where the pond stood.

Touching the boards of the old wooden barns.

Feeling the warmth of welcoming arms.

I remember ... a retreat from the world.

Ribbon That Binds Us

Love is the alchemy of human intimacy,

A beautiful, stretching thing of the heart.

Love is the ribbon that binds us together.

It is the language of the cosmos, the backbeat of the
Universe.

Love is the vibration of Spirit to reach inside of us

And shake our soul.

Shining Stars

How do we raise shining stars that are already in the sky?

Will them to the ground or give them wings to fly?

Dull their brightness or let them glimmer from on high?

A child grows in the wink of any eye.

What they become will signify,

Giving meaning to life as it passes by.

Sisters

Snuggling together on a bed, listening to naptime stories

Making each other eat mud pies made especially for them

Having a contest to see who can swing the highest while pretending to touch the clouds

Walking together to and from school, carrying books, and sharing schoolyard tales

Creating Barbie Land while cautiously waiting for the Giant to come home from work

Splashing in the pool, playing mermaid games, and diving for coins

Sharing clothes and makeup and future dreams

Helping each other grow into womanhood, careerhood, wifehood, motherhood, and grandmotherhood

Watching our own children and grandchildren become sisters.

Success

Success is measured not by the clicking of time, but by the places and faces of those we've touched,

Not by the what, but by the where and the who.

All the trappings will fade away,

But the remembering will remain.

Support

I can walk beside you and hold your hand;

But I cannot stand in your shoes.

I can look into your eyes and image myself seeing the world as you do;

But I cannot climb into your soul.

I can provide a shoulder for you to rest on;

But I cannot be your courage.

We each have our own path to take,

Our own joy to spread and burdens to carry.

I hope I can share yours;

For I need you to share mine.

WBFF

With you, I can be myself, sharing joy and sorrow.

Because of you, I'm a better person, going outside myself.

From your eyes, I see the reflection of who I want to be.

Friends, we laugh and share and care, dreaming of what tomorrow will bring.

Welcome Home

My childhood home, with its open stance, is ready to swaddle me once again.

But, images of the past impose on my present,

Not really now and not really then,

A scene that's half exposed and redolent.

What's real is left to my brain to sort through,

For my heart still sings its youthful refrain.

Old and new overlay to form my view,

Like looking through a new window in an old frame.

Bottled up waiting for me to return, some things remain

    breeze that's moist

    yearned-for voice

    familiar background noise

Some things are left behind and can never be the same

    wishes made once upon

    presence of my father now gone

    family and friends that have moved on

The bittersweet taste of a repast of content,

An anchor when I'm feeling alone,

A tonic when I'm feeling spent,

A welcome home.

FAVORITE THINGS

Heart of the Home

It is not blood and muscle that beats nonstop,

But an oak table with sturdy legs and a scratched top.

It collects memories of a life in contrast,

Long ago conversations with those who have passed.

Late night talks of moving on

Drinking black coffee just after dawn

Making life-changing decisions over a cry

Sharing a meal of gumbo and pecan pie

Homework to pack one more fact into an overworked brain

Kids making projects destined for fame

Discussing past hurts of a love forlorn

A place where new dreams are born

Life of Fat Cat

My fat cat does not sit on the mat;

She sits wherever she wants.

My fat cat does not come when I call;

She responds only to the Treat Bag Shake.

My fat cat is not a feline;

She's really a fat Chihuahua in a cat suit.

My fat cat does not move out of the way;

She makes me step around her.

My fat cat does not do tricks;

She gets me to feed her in the middle of the night.

My fat cat does not meow;

She wails loudly at the bottom of the stairs when I'm
trying to sleep.

My fat cat is not my pet;

She is the master, and I am her faithful servant.

The Magic Garden

Showers of magic transformed the night,

Turning the garden into a lover's delight.

The fountain's mist of silver and blue

Hid secrets only lovers knew.

The yellow stars drifted high

Against the deep, covering sky.

Petals fell to the ground;

Colors descended without a sound.

Lovers walked hand and hand

To ballads played by invisible bands.

The soft, green grass they danced upon,

Their rhythmic sways held back the dawn.

A tender kiss, the lightest touch,

Hands were held in golden clutch.

Eyes exchanged red desire;

Hearts burned with lusted fire.

The Magic Garden still calls to me

To enter a world only lovers see.

Memories

In the stillness of slumber, fragments of the day are slowly drifting down.

Some will flutter by, not stopping to rest or refuel,

Eager to be on their way to the next destination.

Others will remain momentarily;

Maybe they will remain if conditions are favorable.

The rest—a special few—will nestle up close,

Hoping to become a memory.

Office Cadence

Didn't wake 'til half past eight;
Now I'm really running late.
Ring ring
Tap tap
Blah blah blah blah

Meeting went on way too long;
Need some coffee black and strong.
Ring ring
Tap tap
Blah blah blah blah

It's already well past noon;
Better get some work done soon.
Ring ring
Tap tap
Blah blah blah blah

These four walls are closing in;
Overhead lights are getting dim.
Ring ring
Tap tap
Blah blah blah blah

If I keep on running behind;
It'll really be a dead line.
Ring ring
Tap tap
Blah blah blah blah

NEW ORLEANS

Alive Oak

Silvery hair hanging down,

Brown flesh that's stretched and crackled with age,

Arms, long and heavy, extend into the earth and back up,

Embellished with green jewels.

A timeless beauty of majestic elegance,

A portal into another realm,

Seer of good and evil,

The passing of time is embedded in its core.

"Come," it calls to me, "come closer. I have secrets to tell but no one is listening..."

"I will," I whisper, "I will."

Slowly, very slowly, vibrations rise from its soul, up to the tips of its leaves, and out into the world.

City Park

Over the stone bridge I did cross

Live oaks stretch a canopy of moss

Into another world I did step

Where my past and my present gleefully met

An ancient park that generations bind

Of an earlier time it does remind

With flashes of memories all around

Snatches of my childhood to be found

This remembering fulfills a constant need

As time rushes life to greater speed

By treasures of nature in the garden to stroll

Treasures of man for all to behold

Flying horses dance on the round

Coffee and donuts can always be found

Grecian structures to explore

Children squealing to ride one more

Merry in the trees lights do reveal

A land where childhood characters are real

Steel track ride threads sunlight's hair

Pieces of crust with the fowl to share

Water nymphs and seraphs to adore

Feet that paddle far from shore

When sun sends out its last ray

My childhood self wants me to stay

It must wait 'til I return

To be complete we will yearn

Holding on to times of yore

Fearful we will meet nevermore

French Quarter

Café du Monde, waiting for a seat

Anticipating a beignet and coffee treat

Street musicians playing jazz beats

Dancers accompanying them with their feet

Mule-drawn carriages on cobblestone streets

Smell of stale beer mixed with heat

Jackson Square art that's delightfully offbeat

Tin Man offers his silvery greet

Central Grocery muffulettas for something to eat

Stop at Aunt Sally's for praline sweets

On the Moon Walk for a river retreat

Riverboat whistles with the beat

At the Vieux Carré, where old and new meet

A must-go place to feel complete

Jasmine Night

Sip, sip—the jasmine shares

Sweet scents of a summer's night

Encircling lovers with fragrant delight

Drip, drip—the jasmine glistens

Moisture gathers on concrete steps

Forcing nimble lovers to step light

Dip, dip—the jasmine dances

Weaving in and out of the trellised way

Hiding lovers out of sight

King Cake

You sweet ring of royal divine,

Purple, green, and gold—how you shine!

Whether covered with frosting or packed with filling,

A delicious masterpiece that's oh so thrilling.

A royal prize baked inside,

I think I can spy where it's trying to hide.

What a heavenly, epicurean delight,

I long to savor you, bite after bite.

Your taste will linger on my lips,

Long after it's settled on my hips.

Mardi Gras

Controlled chaos at its best

Time for revelers to regress

A New Orleans' party with no rest.

All hail, all hail, Mardi Gras is here!

Where locals and tourist forsake care

Children prancing here and there

Anticipation in the air.

All hail, all hail, Mardi Gras is here!

Barricaded streets lined with fans

Colorful floats and marching bands

All the food and libations y'all can stand.

All hail, all hail, Mardi Gras is here!

King and Queen ride on high

Float riders gliding by

Beads, doubloons, and trinkets fly.

All hail, all hail, Mardi Gras is here!

Reverence to the River

Broad and stout, muse of rhymesters and artists

So, it glows

Buoying boats from foreign ports that patiently wait their turn

So, it shows

Confined by the levee

So, it flows

A good place to catch the breeze

So, it blows

Tides that rise and fall with the moon

So, it grows

Brown churning water carrying sediment from upstream

So, it goes

Currents that scare even the strongest swimmers

So, it bows

Carry my ashes away and mixed them with the world

So, I'll know

River Lights

As a child, I watched the lights dancing with the current.

The river carried them, with my childhood dreams, to faraway places.

Now, I am but a visitor here, a traveler pausing to rest.

I wonder where those lights have gone that once floated by.

SPECIAL TIMES

Autumn

Autumn has once again touched the Forest of Time and left its brilliant mark.

The Tree, which hangs over the River of Fate, cleaves to the fact that the cycle of seasons will continue.

It has been through all this before.

A comforting thought.

The Wind of Change ensures that the oldest, weakest leaves depart first.

The Tree, desperate to protect its remaining leaves, grips even tighter.

But, as the Wind of Change demands, even the last leaf must fall.

Before the Rain Comes

Clouds huddle together as if planning something sinister.

Birds hurry their seed gathering and return to their hatchlings.

Insects fly in erratic patterns, unsure if their wings can withstand the droplets.

Children change into swim clothes and prance around the yard, summoning nature's water park.

Adults rush to close windows, gather precious belongings and scurry inside.

Plants, eager for a drink, open to the idea that life-giving water is coming soon.

G. Allen

Easter Gathering

Feet pattering before dawn

Eggs for gathering on the lawn

Colored wrappers litter the floor

Friends and family at the door

Blond-haired girl in daffodils

Boys with toys causing a shrill

Sparks of sunlight fill the air

Making memories to share

In the Early Morning

Why are you up so early?

I can hear you fussing, waking me from a sound sleep.

Do you not realize what time it is?

You know I love you, but I really must get my rest.

I don't need to feed you or change you or soothe you.

And, you're certainly not welcome in my bed.

I do enjoy you, as long as you stay outside in your nest and keep the chattering low.

In the Evening

The day's echoes are fading away.

Long shadows are reaching for the edge of darkness,
pulling at a blanket of repose.

Day flowers pull back their scents and retreat into
themselves, beckoning for a morsel of gratitude.

Brisk evening air stirs, sweeping away the day's
commotion.

Moisture mixes with the remnants of the day,
producing a restorative tonic.

Memory Tree

On an unassuming plastic tree,

Adorned with beads of red and gold,

And decorated with handmade bows,

Hang precious memories:

Pinecones sprinkled with glister,

Handprints hanging from strings,

Reminders of trips near and far,

Ornaments from those so dear.

Sitting at the very top—

Reigning over it all—

Is a tattered, well-loved Christmas angel

Guarding the treasures below.

New Year's Resolutions

May my mind be sharp, free from old patterns that dull my thoughts.

May my vision be fresh and clear, unobstructed by the fog of past regrets and future expectations.

May my body be agile, to nimbly weave through life's obstacles.

May my spirit carry forth the brightness of hope, so I can shine a light on tomorrow.

NATURE

Blackbirds

A flock of blackbirds came to visit today.

I saw them while looking through the window,

And pondering the happenings of the day.

They feasted at the feeder and flounced around the yard,

Squawking and cackling with much to say.

Shiny black feathers flashing purple in the sun,

Long tail folded like arms that pray,

Their bright yellow eyes sending shrewd glances,

Inviting me to join their soiree.

Then, without regret or regard, they took to the air,

Leaving me to wonder about their stay.

Some days I wish I, too, were a bird,

That I could fly away.

Cherry Trees

I see you, watching me at my desk,

Beckoning me with teasing branches to come outside,

Greeting me when I come home,

In spring, showing off with snowy petals,

In summer, hiding the nesting birds,

In fall, taunting the bus stop children with discarded leaves,

In winter, dancing with the wind.

Cherry trees—marking the seasons of my life.

Clear Cutting

A fresh wound on the earth

Tugging at my heart

For what was

And what will not be.

Left to itself,

It will heal

And call back flora and fauna.

But man

Must impose his righteousness

With inept superiority.

Deadhead

Tiny, shriveled, brown, and bent,

Its once tender rose blossom is now spent.

Nothing is left but a deadhead.

It must be removed

For blossoming to improve.

Nothing to do but deadhead.

Still, something lingers inside its core,

A promised seed of a rose bush once more.

Nothing that holds life can really be dead.

G. Allen

Death of a Boxwood

You're okay, just a little brown.

Maybe that's your way of showing a frown.

As soon as it rains, you'll be fine.

Then, once again, you'll shine.

I'm watering you and spraying you;

What else can I do?

What more do you want from me?

This is not how it's supposed to be!

I'll prune you down, remove the bad.

Then you won't look so sad.

In no time you'll be just fine;

You'll be full, green, and back to divine.

I'm so sad; you're not growing.

In fact, more brown is showing.

I waited too long, applied the wrong spray.

It's my fault you must pay.

Whether you stay or go, it's okay.

I'll accept it either way.

We all have our own time and space,

Others waiting to take our place.

That's the way it should be.

Who wants to be stuck here and never be free?

Downsizing

I grieve for you,

For what is left of your life:

A sad stump,

Still trying to support the limbs and leaves,

That are now gone,

Taken away by the swift, unyielding edge of the saw.

The Faces of Fire

What face will you show today?

One corralled for good or going astray?

Soft and genteel, a servant of man

Or fierce and uncontained, with a scorching plan?

Will you light birthday candles on a cake

Or leave destruction in your wake?

Be a fire in the hearth to warm the soul

Or wildfires burning out of control?

Produce a tasty meal on the grill

Or have an insatiable appetite to burn for the thrill?

A fickle friend with many graces.

Like people, you have many faces.

A destructive power that causes strife

And gives an old forest new life.

Fighting the Wind

I could fight the wind,

Surge against its indiscriminate blows,

Push myself forward, forward,

Pressing on despite its show.

But sometimes it's nice to let the wind win,

Let my body sway to and fro,

Feel the air washing my face,

Allow my mind to drift and flow.

Great Smoky Mountains

Not gaudy, sharp, foreboding, and cautioning,

But ancient, weathered, gentle, and confident,

Like steppingstones a giant could use to traverse a river,

Like multicolored bread, folded onto itself, drizzled with wisps of mist,

Like a herd of camels trying to hide behind a fence,

Like the rocks on the shoreline in a sailor's worst dream,

Like folds of a rumpled bed after a fitful night's sleep,

Like a field of pregnant women, stretched out on their backs,

Like the rise and fall of a poem that rolls off the tongue.

Hummingbird, Hummingbird

Hummingbird, hummingbird, where are you?

I'll know summer is here when your colors glisten true;

I wait on you to make your debut.

Hummingbird, hummingbird, the feeder is up.

Its sweet nectar will fill your cup;

Now is the time for you to sup.

Hummingbird, hummingbird, you're finally here.

I do so treasure having you near;

The return of a friend so dear.

Hummingbird, hummingbird, why do you fight?

Such a fierce temper in one so slight;

Jousting that rivals that of a knight.

Hummingbird, hummingbird, don't you know?

I do adore your acrobatic show;

Wings flashing in sunlight's glow.

Hummingbird, Hummingbird, why must you leave?

When you're off to your winter reprieve;

Your absence I will grieve.

Longleaf Pine

Allow me to gather your discarded needles from which I will make crafty things.

Do not be envious, for they cannot compare with your tall and stately grace.

I only try to capture your wafts of magic with my hands.

Nobel Fight

Tumultuous bands of power, gathered by the storm, unleash wind and rain.

The tree bends to the storm's whims, forcing its branches to wildly swing.

Despite a fight to maintain an upright stance, the tree leans uncomfortably forward.

A brief interlude, the winds calm; the pelting rain turns to a quiet drizzle.

A respite as the storm readies for the next round.

Hope rises in the tree, lulling it into a sense of forgiveness.

Once more, the storm belts out nefarious swirls of increasing might.

Forbidden to rest; the tree summons all its strength to fight this formidable foe.

Bent and battered, it tries to straighten itself.

This time, leaves are torn away; bark is stripped off and cast aside.

Its elegant branches now hang torn and shredded.

In the storm's one last mighty blow, the tree's once-towering trunk snaps and shatters in groaning agony, sending shards of once-alive pulp flying.

What a noble fight!

The tree has yielded to the storm.

But, no matter the victor, in the end—the wind and the rain, like the tree—will be absorbed by the Earth.

Orange Glow

A magical orange glow shines from the horizon, staining the sky pink.

Silhouettes of tall pines stand guard.

The light is slowly fading, giving way to night.

As I witness this magical end of day,

I'm reminded how finite I am in this infinite world.

Day's end here is only the beginning somewhere else.

Point of View

I prefer demure posies growing on a vine,

Or pansies with faces that quietly shine.

You grow flowers that are bright and gaudy,

Dr. Seuss flora looking rather bawdy.

I have my favorite flower;

You have yours;

And, we are both right.

Tall pine forests make me sated,

While desert landscapes look harsh and jaded.

You prefer arid places,

Cactus-filled deserts with open spaces.

I have my sanctuary;

You have yours;

And, we are both right.

Butterflies on a bush I would rather see,

For I want to scamper when they land on me.

Tiny house spiders one can hardly spy,

Make your courage go awry.

I have my bug phobia;

You have yours;

And, we are both right.

Shelby's Tree

You're there for me when I go for my evening walk,

Encouraging me to go one more lap.

For a while I was worried;

The drought seemed to be wearing on you.

I wanted to stop and give you water,

But you're not mine.

It seems you struggled when you were a sapling,

Trying to get a foothold on life.

You kept at it and didn't give up.

Your pink flowers remind me of your namesake,

Who left this world much too young.

Now, you grow for her.

Sunrise on the Beach

Seagulls' squawking quiets the chattering in my head

Sticky breeze cleanses my body

Wet, heavy sand lightens my steps

Shells cluttering the beach clears the debris from my heart

Rising sun in my eyes keeps me focused on what's important

Up a Tree

I would like to join you boys up a tree,

Sit on the thickest branch,

Wave at cars passing by,

Help the little ones who can't climb up on their own.

But, who would fill the bucket that you lower down
when you want more food?

Weeds

Survivors of the plant world, warriors of the lawn,

Providing a livelihood to which some are drawn.

Many try to send you away,

Whether pulling you by hand or killing you with spray.

To me you're green and growing and cover the mud,

With your broad leaves and tiny buds.

What I see is not a pest,

But nature's variety at its best.

We are all weeds just trying to grow,

In a world obsessed by homogeneity and show.

What Birds Say (When You're Not Around)

Mockingbird sitting alone in a tree:

"I can't find a mate so blind dating for me."

Bluebird to Mockingbird as they first meet:

"Hold on, you're not blue, but you can tweet."

Mockingbird's response to get her to stay:

"I'm really blue, just prematurely gray."

Mockingbird shows Bluebird his nesting box:

"This is my pad; it really rocks."

Bluebird starts to build her nest:

"Looks like another female's been here; what a mess!"

Mockingbird trying to make them a pair:

"I was just showing her directions, I swear."

Bluebird is nesting in all kinds of weather:

"Hatching this egg gives me a pain in my tail feather."

Bluebird to Mockingbird when the egg starts to hatch:

"I was beginning to think we were a mismatch."

Bluebird to herself while fetching more food:

"The worm I just gave Baby Blue, he's already chewed."

Bluebird to Baby Blue, who's learning to fly:

"Flap your wings dear and try not to cry."

Baby Blue soaring with new found glee:

"I'll be okay if I just don't hit a tree."

Baby Blue at the birdbath on a hot day:

"Left wing pit, right wing pit. Now I can play."

Baby Blue at the feeder throwing bird feed:

"I hate when we get cheap bird seed."

Baby Blue to his buddies giving them a ribbing:

"HAWK! CAT! HUMAN! No, just kidding."

Bluebird as Baby Blue leaves the nest:

"That chirping was driving me crazy. Now I can rest."

93

White Oak

Oh, great white oak tree,

Why must you shed rusty leaves

After I just raked?

Oh, great white oak tree,

Winter Mourn

On this cold and frosty morn, sky foreboding and gray,

A reason to recapitulate, remembering brighter and warmer days.

Though I remain wrapped in comfort, at home, tucked away,

I can't help but mourn for the light-hearted touch of summer's friendly rays.

INSIGHTS

G. Allen

End of the Pond

Before,

I would jump into the deep end of the pond,

Delightfully anticipating the unknown,

Head first, eyes closed, body long and extended,

Knowing the bottom was far below.

Later,

I still jumped into the pond, but at the shallow end,

Analyzing the known and unknown,

Feet first, eyes open, body held tight,

Avoiding the bottom at all costs.

Now,

I splash on the shoreline of the pond,

Enjoying the view,

Barely getting my ankles wet,

Feeling the bottom against my feet.

Frustration

Running fast in a circle, chasing something

I cannot grasp.

Better to lie down and rest,

Hoping it goes away,

Or finds me.

I wish the path were clearer, like steps

To bake the perfect cake.

I poke, I prod, I probe, I plead, I placate …

Nothing.

All my efforts fall flat.

Gifts

Its opaque walls

Come in many shapes and forms,

Invisible strings

Slowly pulling at the soul,

Binding spirit into a clandestine contract.

Life's ultimate challenge—to find them

Within ourselves.

We are all born

With what we need.

Gratitude

Not an island vacation,

    but a soak in the tub.

Not a romantic dinner,

    but good takeout.

Not an entourage of friends,

    but drinks with my bud.

Not a perfect child,

    but I didn't have to shout.

Not an endless party,

    but a nice weekend trip.

Not running a marathon,

    but walking a mile.

Not a fairytale mate,

    but a good relationship.

Not an extravagant gift,

    but a friendly smile.

Hall of Records

I journeyed to a great hall of records; its end I could not see.

Massive white columns flanked its sides, supporting a ceiling of the sky.

Endless shelves held leather-bound books, each a book of life.

I found my book and began to read, to discover my destiny.

What I found were past accounts and pages to be written.

Embossed on the cover were these words, shining in gilded splendor:

Today is but a whisper of time in the great wheel of life.

Each life is special—fragile yet strong—
blossoms in the field.

We are all interwoven, threads in the tapestry of
humanity.

We are special, with purpose and intent,

Born to serve and be served,

We are to learn, to grow, to take part
in the dance of life.

The roles we play are written,
but the outcomes are for each to craft,

A sprinkle of time to carry forward.

Be kind, be fair.

Do not worry about life's trials, for they give strength and meaning.

Journey

It is not the end of the road where we find ourselves,

But along the way.

When we get to that cherished prize,

We discover that the end is just the beginning of
something else.

The goal was a mere distraction.

For the end wasn't the purpose,

But the journey itself.

Jumping to Conclusions

Ah, Conclusions, my favorite beast.

Always there, your arms wide so I can safely jump to you,

Saving me from evolutionary lessons I don't need to relearn,

Ready to protect me, comfort me, confirm my steadfast beliefs.

You never challenge me, never demand my self-reflection or personal growth.

You reinforce the concrete walls of my mind I erect to keep my ideas and self-identity intact.

You keep out the relentless hounds of reality that chomp at the perimeter, threatening to destroy what

I've carefully built over a lifetime of assumptions.

As the years wear on, you seem to have taken on a life of your own.

Growing increasingly large, fear is the fount at which you feed.

Now I wonder—who serves whom?

Your arms, once reassuring, are becoming increasingly uncomfortable, threatening to strangle me.

Maybe, just maybe, I'm outgrowing you.

You will never leave me, self-preservation will see to that, but...

I can adjust your arms to let in more light.

I can loosen your grip to allow my mind more freedom to consider other possibilities.

I can stop and think for myself.

I can challenge you with other, new ideas, keeping you in your place.

Lessons I Learned from Painting the Walls

If you can't reach what you need to, get a ladder that's tall.

Nothing's perfect, and neither are the walls.

Some things can't be fixed, but caulk and spackling can smooth things out fine.

If the project seems overwhelming, do one thing at a time.

Having the wrong equipment is not a fatal flaw; that's what hardware stores are for.

Don't focus on falling, or you will end up on the floor.

Get help when needed; rely on others' good graces.

Start with what you know, and the rest will fall into place.

Determination, and a good brush, will lead to success.

Stay balanced, or you'll truly have a mess.

Life is Messy

Sometimes the sticks we gather

To erect our dreams or the life we think we need

Gets disrupted by forces unseen or unprepared for

Or by our own hands

Dismantled and rearranged into patterns
unrecognizable but astonishingly familiar

A semblance of a new reality

From which a new life must be structured

Mass Grief

Waves of light souls drift up, away from those of us
anchored in this grief by heavy hearts.

We are groping together in the dark for meaning, an
understanding of the incomprehensible.

We hold on to each other, trying to right ourselves,

Taking solace that our high selves will eventually buoy
us to the surface.

We are not made to dwell here.

Scattered Thoughts

Scattered images

    Snowflakes swirling in my head

Random thoughts

    Melting

Bits of things to do and not do

    Gone before I can catch them

Self-Doubt

I can't!

I never have!

I never will!

I feel doubt lurking around my heart, a black shadow,

A vampire of success filling my head with paralyzing thoughts,

Urging me to tear it up, throw it away, don't show the world that face.

I feel stuck, marching in place to a rhythm not of my own for which I can't master the tune.

I try to cry out, but the rocks in my stomach fall out instead.

Doubt knows me well, always ready to dig into its bag of tricks to pull out just the right blocker.

What if I can't move on?

What if I remain stuck here forever, perpetually circling, unable to proceed?

Give up or get up?

Move aside or move ahead?

My goal shifts; I summon all the strength I can to conquer this vile stalker.

Maybe that's the key.

Maybe that's the purpose of doubt,

To challenge ideas to test their mettle,

To keep egotistical self-assurance in its place.

I can reassure myself with affirmations.

I have courage to take one step at a time.

I will ask for help from all that is seen and unseen.

What once was a boulder will become rubble that I crush so it turns to dust and drifts away.

That Which Bears Fruit

Whether it bears the fruit I think it should,

It bears what it is.

I cannot change the weather that affects the harvest,

But I can tend the tree,

So it produces the best fruit possible.

I cannot control what happens after the fruit is picked,

But I can control the yield in the scope of my limited influence.

To Perform the Dance of Love

Sounds vibrating from the flesh,

Their rhythms fill the room.

Who shall lead and who shall follow?

The push and pull begins.

If he leads, she may not follow;

His power is in her hands.

If she leads, he may not follow;

Her fate is in his hands.

When one steps forward,

The other goes back.

When one steps back,

The other goes forward.

Love is a dance that demands careful attention.

Treasures

Take heed, for you know not what tomorrow will bring.

Today, a moment of time that seems to last but for a second

Can linger evermore in the chambers of the heart.

Savor the moment;

Savor the present;

Taste the bitter and sweet; they balance in the scale of life.

Bear witness to all of life's treasure.

Voyager

So hungry for a crumb of affirmation,

So eager to fill the void where self should be,

Never to fully realize what could be the full blossom of uniqueness.

Fearful to embark on the yon grand journey,

Staying bound in the chains of nascent actualization.

Taste the ripeness of life; drink from the fountain of wakefulness.

Take up the walking stick and venture forth,

For tomorrow's delights await the weary traveler.

Destiny hides in the recess of the storehouse,

Waiting for the ardent voyager.

Wings

These strange, neophytic appendages,

Some days they fit better than others.

Mostly, I don't know what to do with them,

Arrogantly unfurl their magnificence, or keep them
humbly to myself?

Self-effacing is more my style.

They are attractive in a converse way;

Transformation is both restyling and unsettling.

Word Play

Clay in the hands of a writer or language that scorches
the soul?

Touching a loved one from afar or cutting the flesh
without regard?

They can inspire or crush a heart's long-held desire.

Mixed or mashed or smashed or hashed or dashed;

Words can play that way.

ABOUT THE AUTHOR

G. Allen lives in Atlanta, GA, but calls New Orleans home. "I was born and raised in New Orleans. As a third-generation New Orleanian, I still have deep roots in that city and return there as often as I can," she explains. G. Allen indulges her passion for words by writing poetry and, as a technical writer, non-fiction. She has worked as a writer for over 25 years, and prior to that, as a teacher for several years.

Visit the author online:
www.facebook.com/GAllenBooks/